According to John James

A poem with many authors
Edited by Kelvin Corcoran
Cover image by Bruce McLean

Shearsman Books

First published in the United Kingdom in 2018 by
Shearsman Books
50 Westons Hill Drive
Emersons Green
BRISTOL
BS16 7DF

www.shearsman.com

Shearsman Books Ltd Registered Office
30–31 St. James Place, Mangotsfield, Bristol BS16 9JB
(this address not for correspondence)

ISBN 978-1-84861-630-1

i.m. John James 1939–2018

'It's very important
to make your lines
bands of alternating colour
running from one side to the other

these will bind
your poem together
like an egg
& make it exist.'

JJ

It's important that your lines shimmy
R O Y I think blue my best
bands alternate like free radio
from one nation to the next G B

the poem unbound in history
like throwing an egg at a minister of state
another cake unmade
I V I V come back all is forgiven.

KC

It's very important you seize
importance by the scruff and cease
its inveterate finger-wagging in stanzas
howling from the centrally justified margins.

It's crucial you consult the god-long day
outside, covertly squeezing its extremities.
This will grant your lines the requisite limp
and gait light takes to future work, as a bribe.

SP

If the colours are strong
such for example
as the yolk of a fresh egg
your lines can be shorter

the relation of line and
colour is everything
though excess in any direction
does have its place

JH

It's something to walk
the banded fields
as the morning lark
rings forth her appeals

and neglect to remember
how distant we were
in the warm Septembers
of CB2 as it then was.

PR

Select your favourite, say the forest
green, and alternate with white
of silver birch. This prompts meditation
on the following insight:

'If there is always memory
in working-class life
it is because things are
always being taken away'

JT

& still they shine
like in yr face silver studs
on a black leather belt
Kettle's Yard 1981

recalled on the back to the Cold War line
on the gobsmacked anyone's survived line
on the never-ever line the unthinkable line
on the line after this or else another time

AH

It's very important
to make your lines
and stick to them
remembering their names

unless you're as empty
as a wind-swept fen
with a thought in your heart
that sounds like a line of John James

IKP

Unexpected excellent sausage
Contre-jour on a blood & mustard glaze
Like in a painting by Hodgkin
Daubed with sunlight Dijon or Coleman's

Panton St kitchen 1978
Gruff glamour gets the best lines always
& I never had a line in my head
Could sound like a line of John James

JW

The sky is hammered till you can't see the dents
wrapped in blue that perfectly matches itself
The river is full and on the Welsh Backs
the bars are shiny and open

It's a mighty rough road
that never fills up
I'd rather be a canal in Germany
than a sluice here in the South

AD

It's odd to recall
'Sweet the mouth in its quiet'
as you keep an ear open
for what's gone a-fowling

that cawed for its tea
singing Felix's motto
down the long day's stream
& away over the burnet

DR

It's always smart
to wear a vinyl shoe
that expands & yes blowdry
before you put yr foot in it,

if you have to stand up
for a long time – I hope those
other girls are listening –
get shoes that are expandable.

KB

light up with lime relish
the warm smears & caresses
can make it hum
vibrating like an egg

or possibly a rabbit
or Arts Council duck with a cactus
at an English Whitsun festival
or wedding

PH

you could hear it a tiny island in thirty nine
or now as she sags downstream
a brigand at the castle talks clubland electric
a cool fetch ordinary enough to pass

if one's no longer here his belt in the yard
has a smudge of boot polish to keep the rap
unblazoned—taking care of no business
makes the shine go true

GS

of this, look, diolch & diolch again
for lines of alternate colour
like the one drawn that summer
when you rose & left at dawn

as we all still lay asleep
from Talgarth & over
the country line to your love warm
across the grain of the saxon heartland

JG

calm down come down & sit by the edge
some signs of activity radiant
calling back to song calling
an impossible levitation

earth still there turns the turn
Being in the saying
stood gazing willow out in the air
& what narrative to attach

SS

just then a cry
wraps itself round the end of our street
to say there is never
real ending

but only more exfoliations of our cocky
Cambridge meets boho Splott attitude,
swaggering & mouthy
& glimmering the street that hides the ocean

GW

existence well what does it matter?
nights end before they've begun &
the dark stole might perfume your
finger for a whole day

it's all quite groovy in an
anachronistic way: whoever
pinched the belt doesn't even know
the buckle exists

AM

The least explored
There is nothing original in these thoughts
It was the most dangerous thing
The smile so melancholy

Sitting in the setting sun
the whiff of the cigarette
to return to the origin
immersed in the salt

AB

No pattern unworthy of consideration
whether it's hung around for a Platonic month
of Sundays or sparked from a struck flake
stunning upshot of adjustments improvised in the body;

two fingers boogying to the pulse of oceanic
wave bands, one eye on the furniture for the first signs
of mission fatigue: feng shui on a pitching triple-master,
keeping the egg upright on its silver salver.

LD

Honey coloured lines
a little worn like stone
at Corsham Court or
somewhere in England

& thanks for helping
he said just after
as I reached back into
the spirit of Colne spring

TL

Back in 1980 I wrote
'all the best and hoping to hear from you
in bands of alternating colour
running between the lines'

binds it all together
like egg tempera
o tempera o mores
flops from your fingers goodnight

NT

make sure the lines amount to bands of relief
across a piece of card, splitting it & holding the poem
use boot polish over bleach and think… both fresh
& domestic; think ripped curtain over half-peeled fruit

perhaps, not search for the end of the line
settling instead for a dumb setting your feet are used to,
rest and consider that misshapen brick discarded. line.
see it after. & i'll see you after, writer and collector.

CC

it's the significance of
expression steers
authenticity as bind to
switching

at least one mistake
– lipstick –
grazes the stirrups
appropriation gives up

LK

under siege and close to starving
they throw the carcass of their last ox
over the walls of the fortress
their attackers inspect it and leave

light on your feet
weighed with intent
make your lines hungry and free
beams left exposed reflect light

CY

It is important that lines   poems   people
greet, their lives, edges making shapes sensual
expectations of the frenzied intimacy
of silhouettes, waves lining coastlines,

trainwheels on rail-lines: no lines in nature:
rather the fractal melding of conjunctions
of faces, you and me, trees and the sun,
lines of attraction, kiss, kiss.

RVD

Settle your profession of art wrinkles,
motor yak hew version
curling dance foible and later cling to rota
rift minor design tooth;

dud wise, most blithe in marsh heather
roped urn merry holding
avoid all elk in glen – extend roll
permanent rake system next ... that's it.

ML

All such to life consuming
  as all were true
in air passing and lifted
  besprent with dew

Nor lavish nor in unison
  even at the shore
for giving its world over
  for this and more

JHP

A little heap of fresh sawdust
This is a porous surface, made of words
The spreading fragility of our love
With all its openings windows apertures leaks

We can be other than we are
And always hoping
Confront the atmosphere,
unprotected by sheets of glass

RH [author of none of these lines]

'It's very important
to make your lines
bands of alternating colour
running from one side to the other

these will bind
your poem together
like an egg
& make it exist.'

JJ

Acknowledgements

The editor thanks Rhiannon Munro for permission to use the first eight lines from John James's *A Theory of Poetry*. The following each contributed two quatrains to *According to John James*:

Kelvin Corcoran	Simon Smith
Simon Perril	Geoff Ward
John Hall	Anthony Mellors
Peter Riley	Anthony Barnett
John Temple	Lyndon Davies
Alan Halsey	Tony Lopez
John Wilkinson	Nick Totton
Ian Patterson	Chris Cornwell
Andrew Duncan	Linda Kemp
Denise Riley	Cliff Yates
Karlien van den Beukel	Robert Vas Dias
Peter Hughes	Mark Leahy
Gavin Selerie	J.H. Prynne
John Goodby	Romana Huk

Pages set by John Hall

www.ingramcontent.com/pod-product-compliance
Lightning Source LLC
Chambersburg PA
CBHW021947040426
42448CB00008B/1274